YOUR KNOWLEDGE HAS VALUE

Mario Pesch

Mortgage-backs are the root of all evil

A cat fight

GRIN Verlag

Bibliografische Information der Deutschen Nationalbibliothek:

Die Deutsche Bibliothek verzeichnet diese Publikation in der Deutschen National-
bibliografie; detaillierte bibliografische Daten sind im Internet über http://dnb.d-
nb.de/ abrufbar.

Imprint:

Copyright © 2010 GRIN Verlag GmbH
Druck und Bindung: Books on Demand GmbH, Norderstedt Germany
ISBN: 978-3-656-52087-0

This book at GRIN:

http://www.grin.com/en/e-book/164363/mortgage-backs-are-the-root-of-all-evil

Mortgage-backs are the root of all evil

Cat Fight – The "Yes"-side

Mario Pesch

F506 Commercial and Investment Banking, Fall Term 2010

11/03/2010

MORTGAGE-BACKS ARE THE ROOT OF ALL EVIL – YES!

Mortgage-backs securities (hereafter MBSs) could be seen of the root of all evil. To understand this statement it is important to define "evil" related to MBSs as well as the use of MBSs.

"Evil" refers to the results of the financial crises that were strongly related to MBSs. Especially this incorporates the money losses of investors, the diminishing trust in rating agencies as well as banks and the overall downtown of the economy.

MBSs are financial securities that are created out of a pool of prime mortgages. This process is called securitization and banks establish special-purpose-vehicles (SPV) to collect payments from the mortgage holders and then pay fractional streams of interest to the investors, i.e. the holders of the MBSs. In general, MBSs provide banks with the ability to get loans off their balance sheet, i.e. to diversify the default risk to a higher number of investors. In the years before the burst of the housing bubble this regular use of MBSs has changed. However, it can be shown, that the characteristics of MBSs supported an industry environment, which led to the creation of a housing bubble and its burst.

To understand the reason why MBSs have become "the root of evil", one has to understand the strong relation of the market for MBSs between rating agencies, investors and banks/financial institutions.

Rating agencies are related to create this dangerous environment for two main reasons. First, they did not have or they did not want to spend enough time to evaluate most MBSs. This happened due to conflicts of interest, created by making profit for each finalized rating and at the same time providing credible ratings to the public. However, the rating agencies are paid by the banks, therefore making profit can be seen as the more favorable goal. Second, the rating agencies did not have accurate rating tools to evaluate MBSs or simply used definitions of AAA-ratings that lead to misunderstandings for the investors. From this follows that the expected risk exposures have been systematically underestimated. For instance, rating agencies gave an AAA-rating for the senior tranches within a securitization bundle, due to the fact that those will be paid first, not taking into account that the overall risk of the securitized assets could be high. These reasons increased the risk connected to MBSs because the public information in the markets has been wrong.

Solely relying on evaluations from rating agencies, which have been a reliable indicator in the past, investors have been convinced that MBSs are close to the risk of highly rated corporate bonds or even government bonds. This behavior can be seen as rational from investors' perspective, because of two reasons. First, banks "created" so many different types of MBSs that investors put their trust in "experienced" evaluators, i.e. the rating agencies, and second, products became so complicated that sometime it would take a mathematician to explain them. The following high investments in these assets lead to unexpected portfolio risks (investors, like money-market funds or pension funds have been attracted by MBSs because they need to follow restrictions that only allow them to invest in AAA-rated assets).

However, researchers argue that bad investment choices within an asset group would not harm the total financial sector. Given the very high losses in the MBS-market, it still seemed manageable, given the overall size of U.S. and world debt markets. The financial and economic crisis, beginning with the burst of the housing bubble, was more a result of the behavior of banks/financial institutions, which ignored their original business model.

Originally banks acted as financial intermediaries, meaning to take deposits in order to deal in credits. Governmental regulations made sure, that banks meet certain capital requirements to secure that depositors will receive their money any time they request it. In the years before the crisis, MBSs worked as a tool for banks to by-pass these regulations. Additionally banks did not only use MBSs to spread their risk, as intended, rather they invested in MBSs themselves. Equipped with the possibility to move loans off the balance sheet and to invest in high rated MBSs, banks could give out more loans than they could have without MBSs. As long as the market was stable, the banks could increase their profits. The chance of high profits could be seen as a reason for the observed growth rates of subprime-MBSs. At the same time, the quality of subprime-MBSs has been deteriorating monotonically every year since 2001.

With the downturn of the markets and the losses of MBSs, banks faced two major problems. First, banks had to handle huge losses on their own positions of MBSs and related derivatives. Second, the funding of long-term mortgage assets relied on the ability to roll over short-term financing sources. With the breakdown of the market and the resulting doubts about counterparties' creditworthiness, related to exposures to the MBSs-market, financial firms had to deal with a severe liquidity squeeze. Finally, many financial institutions have not been able to survive this hazardous environment.

To conclude, MBSs could be seen as "the root of all evil" because these financial instruments could be misused to by-pass capital requirement regulations and could not be evaluated accurately and therefore created misleading information in the financial markets. With the downturn of the housing market, these reasons can be seen as the root for the financial and economic crisis.

Bibliography

- Acharya & Richardson (2009). Causes of the Financial Crisis. Critical Review 21(2–3), pp. 195–210.
- Alessandri & Haldane (11/2009). Banking on the State. Bank of England, pp. 1-30.
- Jereski, Laura (1/1993). Alice in Mortgageland. Forbes, Vol. 151 Issue 5, pp. 46-48.
- Vink, Dennis & Thibeault, André E (Summer 2008); ABS, MBS, and CDO Pricing Comparisons: An Empirical Analysis. Journal of Structured Finance, 14, 2, pp. 27-45.
- W.W. Lang, J.A. Jagtiani (2010). The Mortgage and Financial Crises: The Role of Credit Risk Management and Corporate Governance. Atlantic Economic Journal, 38, pp. 295–316.